Magickal Se

Attract Love, Sex and
Ancient Secrets and Words of Power

Damon Brand

Acknowledgements

Grateful thanks to Adam and Gordon for access to images from the private collection. Thanks also to Gordon for contributing updated information.

CONTENTS

How Does Magickal Seduction Work?

If there is somebody you have longed for, the magick in this book can bring that person to you. If you want casual sex with attractive people, the magick here works. If you're looking for true love, this magick can set the wheels of passion in motion.

True seduction is the art of attracting the people who will please you the most, sexually and emotionally. At its best, seduction is also a gift to the one you seduce, because you are the one that will please them the most, sexually and emotionally.

You can use magick to seduce for fun, and so long as you are a kind and generous lover, you won't get any backlash from the magick. You can also seduce to find yourself a long-term lover or a life partner.

Whatever your gender or sexual orientation, magickal seduction is a powerful way to bring pleasure into your life.

Whether you're looking for casual sex or true love, magickal seduction can break through blocks, inspire attraction and magnetize a couple together.

I have used seduction magick for decades. It didn't start working consistently until I was in my late twenties when I discovered the techniques explained in this book. Then it worked extremely well.

The magick has also been tested extensively by women and in homosexual situations, with the same powerful results.

I have used seduction magick for fun nights of one-off sex with old friends and people I've just met.

I've used it to get many girlfriends and eventually to find my life partner. I have also made some terrible mistakes with seduction magick, but along the way, I have found out what works well, and the mistakes you need to avoid. This means you can avoid such mistakes by following the instructions as set out in this book. You can work with the most powerful magick straight away, and get results.

It should go without saying that this is not a book of deception or coercion. Your aim is not to trick or hypnotize somebody into desiring you, but to shine so brightly that where there is potential for love or lust, it is maximized. The magick works best when you are considerate of the needs and desires of others, rather than trying to force things to go your way. Work with empathy and kindness, and you will get good results.

Where Does This Magick Come From?

I never share magick unless I have found it to work for myself and others. I don't mind whether magick is ancient or modern, so long as it works. The magick presented in this book is partly modern, but the spirits and entities that are employed have been around for a long time.

Just about any ritual you want can be found on the Internet with some searching, but magick that works is a little rarer. Although ancient grimoires are now easily obtained online, most of these books leave out the important instructions for their use.

One of the tasks for modern occultists is to illuminate the process behind the words. If you were to obtain a copy of *The Black Screech Owl* or *The Black Pullet,* you could find some of the magickal words and symbols included in this book. But that is all you would find. I know of several people who have tried to work with the instructions in those books, treating the instructions literally, and unsurprisingly, the magick does not work. However, when you take the time to unravel the secrets hidden in the text, and find other sources that reference practical methods that predated or evolved from those books, you can find out how to actually *work* the magick.

That is what I will give you here: the secret to making ancient magick work in the modern world. The Gallery of Magick have made a commitment to illuminate magick, simplifying the process as far as possible, without reducing the potency of the rituals.

There is almost nothing in this book that we invented from scratch, because the concepts have been in use for centuries. Until recently, they were not widely available. This book will communicate to you exactly how to perform the rituals, what to think, what to feel and how to get the results you want.

Is This Magick Dangerous?

Seduction is not about tricking somebody into having sex with you. Even if sex is all you want, seduction should be an art that benefits all. If you are looking to use people resentfully, treat them as objects and then discard them thoughtlessly, this is not the book for you. This isn't only a moral issue, but a safety issue. Seduction magick is safe so long as you don't create resentment in people. If you use people and make them feel used, they have a direct link back to you, straight through the magick. That can hurt.

The simplest protection is at hand: be kind.

I am not going to be overly moralistic, though, because sex is not inherently unkind, and exploring desire can benefit everybody involved. If you've been flirting with somebody at the office for years, and finally want to get into bed with them, this is the way. Get it done and enjoy it. Kindly and with consent, obviously.

But if you use sex magick to trick somebody who doesn't like you into having sex, then it's unlikely to be good sex, and nobody will feel good in the morning. Such magick is not explored here. This seduction magick can be so much more enjoyable than that.

Even if you want to go off on a rampage of casual sex – and this book can certainly help with that – you should be respectful to those you seduce. If it's going to be casual, don't make promises of a relationship or another date. There's no need to lie. In short, seduce by being truthful and by being yourself. The magick will do the rest.

Equally, if you end up in a relationship as a result of this magick, and then the relationship doesn't work out, end it peacefully. Broken relationships can lead to hatred, anger, and even murder. Do yourself a favor by being kind to those you break up with, especially when the seduction was magickal.

If you follow these simple rules, the magick will not be dangerous.

Although you should be respectful, seduction is not a state where you shape yourself to somebody else's desires. You will never need to beg, whine or plead to get what you want, and everybody gets to have a good time.

Real seduction comes from confidently offering the best of yourself. That sentence contains an important truth, and you would be wise to consider it over and again while working this magick.

Magick can open up perceptions so that people see the beauty, grace, and pleasure you have to offer. You are not seeking conquests, but offering the gift of yourself.

Magick in the Real World

Back in the nineties, I attended a prestigious book launch in London. I'd broken up with a fairly long-term girlfriend, but I was in a good place mentally and emotionally. I was neither desperate to replace her, nor wanting to be alone. This casual confidence is a great state of mind for seduction.

I was aware that I wanted to meet new people, and seduce new people, but rather than being desperate about it, I simply made sure that I went to lots of social events. I decided to use the magick that's explained in this book, to make me generally more attractive to people.

For the first week, I met a lot of interesting people, and there were a few women who seemed to be interested in me, but I didn't pursue it, and neither did they.

At the book launch, I was introduced to a woman who I will refer to only as Z, and she was the most beautiful woman I had met at that point in my life. To my astonishment, she seemed genuinely interested in me.

It was like one of those meetings in a movie, where it's completely obvious that the couple are about to fall in love. I was astonished at how well it was going, because although I am not bad looking, Z was way out of my league. My friends were watching in amused awe, probably wondering when I was going to screw it up.

Out of nowhere, I found myself telling Z that she was the most beautiful woman I'd ever met, and she replied by saying that she found me attractive. I asked her to meet me for lunch the next day, and she agreed, immediately giving me her phone number. She then told me that she had a boyfriend, and wasn't sure what to do about that yet, but that she *did* want to meet me. So, despite the odds, I'd attracted Z. The magick worked.

What followed is the interesting part. I kept drinking and kept talking to her, and partly I was enjoying a massive ego-trip. I wanted my friends to be slightly jealous and to admire me for getting this beautiful woman interested in me. And that was my mistake. Within an hour I was so drunk that I lost my cool, and although my memory of the evening isn't too clear, I know that I made an idiot of myself. Before she left, Z told me that she wasn't going to meet me the next day.

The lesson I learned is that sometimes, when the magick is done, you just need to leave. Often, a seduction goes so well that you go home together and jump into bed that night. Sometimes, though, it's obvious that things have the potential to be more long-term. When that happens, it's a good idea to make an arrangement to meet the person in question at another time. Once that's done, you should leave the social event as soon as you can. If you cannot leave, politely excuse yourself and talk to other people for the rest of the evening. When your magick works, accept that it has worked, and then make sure you don't ruin the power that has been put in place.

Making a future date is often a good idea anyway, if you have the patience. That way, the object of your affection gets to spend a whole night thinking about you before you meet again. There is great power in that.

Even the best magick can be ruined by your own stupidity, impatience or over-enthusiasm. When you've made a date, get out of the way and then turn up for the date. Don't get drunk and show off. Powerful magick wears off quite quickly when you hang around getting unattractively drunk.

This applies even in more formal settings, where there may be no alcohol or drugs involved. Imagine you're at a work conference, and you meet somebody during the lunch break, and then the two of you arrange to meet for dinner. At that point, with the arrangement made, you should excuse yourself and get out of the way. Don't hang around with that person all day. Get out of there and wait until dinner. Then you can work your personal charm all over again.

Magick is only ever one factor in a situation. The magick in this book is so powerful that its effects might shock you, but you still need to apply the best judgment, style, and grace that you can, to make it pay off.

How to Use Love Magick

There are three rituals in this book. The first ritual is aimed at making passion arise in somebody specific. This will work so long as you have some contact with the person. It's not going to work on movie stars unless you happen to be friends with them already. It is ideal in situations where you want a relationship with a specific person, but nothing has happened yet. It can also be used when there is some attraction, but the other party doesn't seem as passionate as you want them to be.

The next part of the book looks at love. There is an extremely powerful ritual for making somebody fall in love with you. Some people try this ritual from the outset, but I recommend using this when there is already some attraction. Ideally, use the first ritual to ignite passion and *then* turn it into love. Be certain you actually want somebody to be in love with you. If they are married, for example, do you really want the fallout that can result from that? It's fine if you do, but go into this with your eyes wide open. The magick works, so don't use it casually.

The final part of the book looks at creating a general aura of attraction around yourself. It takes the opening ritual and modifies it so that you disturb the aura of everybody you meet, making them see you as attractive. Be prepared for strong results from this, because it works fast and it works powerfully.

Since this book was first published, we have received lots of feedback. It has become very clear that to ensure the magick works, you need to read the book thoroughly. Although the magick can be performed quickly and easily, ensure that you have understood exactly what you are meant to do, so that you can be relaxed and confident when performing the magick.

There has also been a rapid growth in online dating. It can be the main way that people seem to meet each other these days. Can the magick work over an app? The magick can make you more attractive, but the attraction is a thousand times stronger when you actually end up in the physical presence of that person. And that is what you're aiming for in the end, anyway. You don't want to stay online forever, so get offline and connect in the real world.

Working with The Power

When you perform magick, you are warned to avoid lusting for results. The reason is that when you perform a ritual, you are effectively asking for something else to do the work for you. You are handing the task over to spirits and powers.

When you do this, you should trust these spirits to do the work. If you keep checking up on them, by wondering about the results, you're showing that you don't trust them, and this can make the whole operation fail. The spirits *will* do what you ask. Show your trust by letting go of your lust for result. Feel grateful that the result will come about and that is all you need to do.

Although this 'handing off' is important, and it should feel as though you've handed the difficult work over to somebody else, you should also do as much as you can in the real world. There's little point in performing an attraction ritual if you spend the next ten evenings at home. There's not much use in performing a love ritual if you won't come into contact with your target.

So, let go of the results – because the hard work is being done for you on a magickal level – but still do everything you can to be the most attractive and available person you can be.

This can be a tricky mental balancing act, but it is the one you must master for magick to work.

I helped a man some years ago, who had gone seven years without having sex. He was desperate, and that makes magick difficult, because magick works best when you have confidence. But I helped him, and he got a date. He was so nervous that he asked me to turn up at the same café and hang around in the background to be on hand in case he needed advice. I went, and I sat nearby and watched closely. It was amusing, but quite sad.

Mistakes and idiosyncrasies in a person can be endearing, but he took this a bit too far. He was not well dressed. He actually had some food stuck in his beard. And he immediately launched into an enraged political tirade, without asking the young woman anything about herself. He kept smiling, which is always important, so I congratulated him for that, but he got almost everything else wrong. I realized at this point that he needed to read some basic books on seduction, dating and relating to people.

If you suspect that this may be a problem for you, then you should do the same. The magick is powerful, but it only works when you are offering the best of yourself. Do not go out looking unwashed, disheveled, drunk, angry, arrogant or standoffish.

Magick is powerful, and it can work seeming miracles, but put the odds on your side by being the best that you can. This is not selling out or deceiving people. The gift of seduction is to be a glory that somebody else can revel in. This doesn't mean you have to lose weight, buy new clothes and so on, but realistically, that sort of thing always helps.

How to Speak the Words

Pronunciation is not overly important when it comes to magick. The words are often Latin or Hebrew in origin. To make it easy I have presented them in capitals, and they can be said as though they are English words.

So, where it says DESK-END-EE-MOOSE AB EYE-RAY, you just use the English sounds for those words, as follows:

DESK is the word **desk**.

END is the word **end**.

EE is like **bee** without the **b**.

MOOSE is the word **moose**.

AB is like **dab** without the **d**.

EYE is the word **eye**.

RAY is the word **ray**.

As you can see, if you read the words in capitals as though they are English, you will get the pronunciation close enough for it to work. After a few moments of working with a word, you should be able to say it easily.

The AH sound is used quite often, so if you see AH know that it sounds like the **a** sound in **ma** and **pa**. As such, the word SAH is just **ah** with **s** at the front. The pronunciation is simple if you take just a few minutes to sound the words out loud.

Also, note that **G** sounds like the **g** in **give** rather than the **g** in **giant**.

In some rituals, the spirit's name is followed by a phonetic pronunciation in parentheses. So, if you see Raziel (RAH-ZEE-ELL), you don't need to say it twice; you just say RAH-ZEE-ELL.

This is all you need to know to get the sounds close enough to work. If you want more details, the *Pronunciation and Spelling FAQ* on The Gallery of Magick website gives examples of how to say the words in a video.

More important than the pronunciation, is the way that you let the words come out of your body. Let the words vibrate from the base of your lungs, through your throat and out of your mouth as though you are speaking them to the horizon. They should not be whispered but allowed to resonate in your throat as they pass out of you.

If you need to work without being heard, you can imagine saying the words, but if you do so, imagine that they are rumbling out of you loudly. This is more effective than merely whispering.

You may want to know what the words mean and what you are calling. The main alchemical rite in this ritual is derived from a ritual that expanded on the workings of *The Emerald Tablet*. I am not at liberty to say more than that, but if you have concerns about this, know that many people have used the magick successfully and without problems. If it were at all dangerous, I wouldn't publish it. The ritual serves only to place you in a position of authority, where you are granted the right to command spirits to work according to your needs.

Ritual 1: Igniting Passion in Another

If you know the person you want to attract, these are the ritual instructions you need. This is widely regarded as the most powerful ritual in the book.

You can perform this at any time of the month, but there are two times that are particularly powerful. If you have limited contact with the person you are aiming to enflame, it is best to begin the ritual on the evening of a New Moon, and perform it for five nights.

If there is already some warmth and friendship between the two of you that seems close to being passion, then the best time to begin is five days before a Full Moon. Perform this for five nights, ending on the Full Moon.

At one point in the ritual, you will be asked to burn three red candles. Never burn a candle unless it is safe to do so. I don't want to sound patronizing, but I know of several occultists who've done simple candle rituals and invited disaster through fire. Candles may seem harmless, but many homes and lives are destroyed each year by fires that started with a candle. Bear in mind that you are lighting a fire inside your home. This may sound overly cautious, but it is a serious point.

In terms of economy, the best way to get three red candles is to buy one and snap it into three pieces. Make sure each candle is set in a holder that keeps it safe and secure.

You need to prepare a magickal ring. This can be

copied from the following drawing. If you prefer you can download it from our website and print it out:

http://galleryofmagick.com/images/

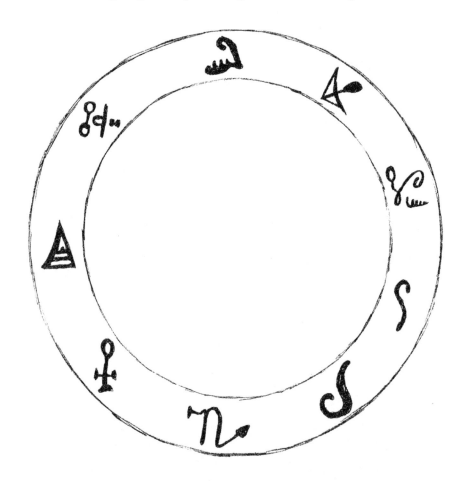

If you do print it out, it helps if you trace lightly over all the symbols yourself, with a black pen. You can use any paper, and this doesn't have to be an elaborate operation. Cut the circle out, and set it aside until you actually begin the ritual.

It helps to have a small block of pyrite. That can

be obtained from many occult suppliers, crystal shops and so on. It looks like this:

If you cannot find pyrite, a small block of any metal will work, with iron being the best. If you cannot get a small block of metal, a stone will do the job. Whatever you use, it should be small enough to fit inside the magick circle that you've drawn.

It is time for the ritual itself to begin. Find some time and space to be alone.

Bathe or shower, as though preparing to have sex with the person you desire.

For best results, find a comfortable place to work without any distractions. You may want to dim the lights or close the curtains if it is daytime. If it is warm enough, and if you find it a lustful experience, perform the ritual naked. Otherwise, dress in a way that makes you feel attractive.

Now take a fresh sheet of paper of any kind, and tear off a small scrap. Make sure there are no straight edges – the scrap should have a torn edge all around. On this, write the name of the person you wish to seduce. Write the name several times, to make a circle. It should look something like this:

Place this scrap of paper face down in the middle of the magickal ring, so that you can no longer see the written name. Now place your pyrite, or other heavy object, over the scrap of paper to hold it in place. Consider that the person you are attracting is now held within the powers of this magickal ring.

Ensure that three red candles are placed nearby, but do not light them yet.

Say the following words out loud:

> I am grateful for all that I have.
> I am humble when I revel
> in the wonders of power.

As you say the first sentence, take a few moments to think about things that you are truly grateful for. This may be the roof over your head, a movie you watched, or a good cup of coffee. Don't try to be grand and impressive, but simply think of recent pleasures that genuinely make you feel grateful. *Feel* the gratitude, rather than thinking about it intellectually.

As you read the second sentence, you are making

a pact. You are promising that when you have the power to seduce with magick, you will be joyously impressed and grateful for the power, but you will not be boastful or arrogant about your abilities. Consider these thoughts as you say the words. Make them feel true as you say them.

If you need to, say these sentences three times each, to make sure you actually feel the words.

Light your three red candles.

Now comes the part of the ritual where you summon up the power of fire, heat, and passion. Say the following words out loud, vibrating them through your throat.

DESK-END-EE-MOOSE AB EYE-RAY

OOT ASK-END-AT ET DESK-END-AT

MOW-TOOS INT-AIR DO-OSS

NO-AH IN-WENT-AH IN LOO-KEM

IN-SEEG-NEH CORP-US
EX ELL-EM-ENT-EES

NONE EST ACK-EE-DENSE

MOON-DUSS IN MEN-SAH
MAY-AH AIR-ANT

MEESK-AIR-EH CUM

LAP-EE-DEE-BOOSE FAIR-UM

ADD KEYE-RULE-UM
WEE-REED-ESS GEM-ASS

ET WHEN-IT ET POST-HACK FOO-TOORA

NONE SUNT OWE-SA MAYA

SPECK-TOE, LOW-KUSS
EST MED-EE-UM

OOT AMB-OOLS IN WEE-AH IG-NISS

TEMP-OAR-RAY MOW-EH-TOUR

This is an alchemical rite, written in Latin. It speaks of the way we can change reality with our will. You do not need to know the meaning of the words, so focus only on the sounds the words make as you say them.

When you have finished speaking, imagine the sun. Imagine it as a vast ball of heat and flame, but then see it shrinking, so that in moments it becomes a star. As the sun shrinks, it moves inside your heart and resides there. Imagine this tiny pinprick of light within your heart, containing all the massive power and heat of the sun.

Don't worry if your imagination is not perfectly clear. All you need to do is imagine that the sun has shrunk and is now a tiny star in your heart.

You should now begin to picture the person you desire and hear their name in your head. You can begin to masturbate at this point, but it is not essential. Masturbation is an extremely potent way to add energy to a working, but it requires some control because you do not want to reach orgasm until later in the ritual. It's your choice, but for the best results, masturbation provides the most potent energy.

For several minutes, picture yourself with the person you desire. Imagine sexual acts and a strong passion and desire between the two of you.

Once you feel that your lust for the person is strong, say these spirit names:

NAH-DESS
SUE-RAH-DISS
MAH-KNEE-NAIR

As you say the words, know that you are summoning spirits of lust. You may sense the spirits' presence upon first uttering the words. Repeat the words two more times, and you should feel a slight change in the atmosphere. If you feel nothing, it does not matter. Simply know that the spirits do come when called.

Visualize an orange-rosy light before you. By calling the spirits, you have summoned them to bring this light.

Picture the person you want to be with inside the rosy light, and picture yourself there as well. Imagine that you are together, kissing, making love. When you can see this and feel the pleasure of it, say the spirit names:

SAH-DARE

PRO-STASS
SOL-AST-AIR

Speak directly to these spirits of lust, with authority, while picturing your target. Repeat these spirit names over and over.

It's vital that you picture yourself in lustful situations with your target. Don't hold back with these images. Picture yourself doing exactly what you desire, and picture your target loving the sex. DO NOT picture your first date, or how you plan to get together. Picture the result, not the process. Picture lustful sex, as though it is happening now. If you are masturbating, take yourself close to orgasm as you picture these lustful acts.

After a minute or two of chanting these names, and building your lust, say the following (but replace N. with the full name of your target.) Remember you are speaking *to* the spirits named above.

Bring me N.
Enflame his/her mind and body
with passion for me,
and you may feed on the energy and
ecstasy of our sex to your satisfaction.

If you are masturbating, continue to picture the object of your affection until you reach orgasm. Wipe a small amount of your sexual fluids onto the scrap of paper in the center of the ring. Not too much, because you will be doing this for five nights.

If you are not masturbating (or if you are

masturbating but can't reach orgasm), simply let the images fade away.

To close the ritual, say the following words, vibrating each word through your throat.

WHEN-AIR-AND-UM IG-NISS
NONE TEAM-AY-OH

ET IG-NISS NONE TOH-LIT

IG-NISS CON-CORD-EE-AM FACK-EAT

This rite affirms that the fire of magick does not harm or destroy, but brings harmony.

Blow out the candles. The ritual is over. Put your magickal implements away where they will not be disturbed until you need them, and do not think about the result you are seeking. To distract yourself you should cook, eat, sing, or talk to a friend, but do not sit around wondering whether the magick will work. The work is done, so get on with something else.

Repeat the ritual for five nights. On the final night, let the candles burn down until they go out – but only if it is safe to do so. Never leave them unattended.

Once the ritual is complete for the last time, roll the scrap of paper up into a ball, then wrap that up in the magickal paper ring you drew. Screw it all up, and bury it somewhere nearby, preferably on your property. If you have nowhere nearby to bury it, there is no urgency to get rid of it – so you don't need to wander the streets at night looking for a suitable place to dispose of it – but within one or two days find somewhere to bury it that is not a graveyard.

When you next see the target of your ritual, act as you normally would, but visualize a veil of white light wrapping itself around that person. Take just a few seconds to visualize this, and then carry on as normal.

It will not be long before you are given a sign that something has changed. The magick has worked and how you deal with it is up to you.

Ritual 2: Turning Attraction into Love

The simplicity of what follows should not be underestimated. If you sense that somebody is attracted to you, this ritual can turn the desire into love.

This works whether or not you have begun a relationship already. You can use the ritual when the person in question is a friend, a casual lover or a more serious partner. It will not work on complete strangers, and it will not work if there is no attraction. If there is no attraction, use other parts of the book to get to that stage first.

The ritual is powerful. Be warned that the results can be so powerful that they are life changing. I am with my life partner as a result of this ritual.

Be careful what you wish for. If you are wise, you will only use a love ritual when you are sure that falling in love will work for both of you. This ritual will work on you as well, making you fall more deeply in love than you already are.

At one point in the ritual, you will call on the angel Haniel. For that, you can print out or copy the following sigil, and have it nearby. Again, it can be found on the website if required. You can use it directly in the book, without printing any physical copy, and that works just as well.

http://galleryofmagick.com/images/

The ritual makes use of powerful spirits that are bound by the powers of the archangel Raziel. Although Raziel can be difficult to contact, by making a call to Arzel (who is an easily contacted angelic *aspect* of Raziel) you make the required connection easily. You will notice that the ritual uses many different calls, with slightly different pronunciations, to make this effective. Don't worry about getting the pronunciation perfect.

Make sure you have the sigil of Haniel nearby

and begin the ritual by evoking Raziel as follows.

In a quiet space, sit or stand facing East, and repeat the phrase:

NAH-KAH EE-AH-OH-EH

Say the words out loud. They are pronounced as written.

NAH sounds like the word **ah** but with an **n** at the beginning.

KAH sounds like **ah** with a **k** at the front.

EE is like **bee** without the **b**.

AH, OH and EH are exactly like the English words **ah**, **oh** and **eh**.

This phrase means something along the lines of, 'I choose to recognize God.' Whatever your beliefs, you probably have some concept of a God, Creator or Universal Power. You can know that you are connecting to the authority of that power. By saying this phrase, you are giving yourself the authority to command spirits, through the power assigned to you by God.

Repeat this phrase until you feel that you are beginning to relax and that your mind is entering a trance-like state. You don't need to be out of your mind; just let yourself relax into a magickal state of mind. The following words are ancient words of power, fragments of psalms and spirit names, and they have been used safely and successfully for centuries. When you feel ready to call on Raziel - it might take two seconds or a few minutes - say the following:

KOH-SUE HAH-REE-EEM TZIL-AH
VAH-ANNA-FEHA ARE-ZELL

ARE-ZELL, ARE-ZELL, ARE-ZELL

ARZ-ALE, ARZ-ALE, ARZ-ALE

ARE-ZAY-ELL, ARE-ZAY-ELL, ARE-ZAY-ELL

I call on thee, Raziel (RAH-ZEE-ELL) in the East
to make me heard by the secret angels of the
universe.

RAH-ZEE-ELL, RAH-ZEE-ELL, RAH-ZEE-ELL.

You may sense a bright white light, or smell the scent of trees, or hear pleasant, calming noises. If you don't feel much or anything at all, don't worry - Raziel is listening. Raziel comes when called in this way, and is working for you. Now say:

Oh mighty Raziel (RAH-ZEE-ELL),
let my voice be heard by
Sisera (SEES-AIR-AH), genius of desire,
and Jazar (JAZZ-ARE), genius who compels love.

I seal this command with the word of power
AH-RAH-REE-TAH).

Say the following, replacing N. with the name of the
one you love:

In the Power of the Names EH-HE-YEAH,
EE-AH-OH-EH ELL-OH-HEEM,
and EE-AH-OH-EH ELL-OH-AH-VAH-DAH-ART
Sisera (SEES-AIR-AH), genius of desire
and Jazar (and JAZZ-ARE),
genius who compels love,
bring me the love and passion of N.
Send my love into his/her heart so
that s/he returns my love.
I command this in the Names of
SHAD-EYE-ELK-EYE
and ADD-OH-NIGH-HA-AH-RETZ.

Gaze at the sigil of Haniel. Say the word 'Eh.' This is
the Greek vowel eta, which sounds like the middle of
the word **set**. It should take two or three seconds to
say this vowel, starting at a high pitch and ending
low. Saying this word ignites the sigil of Haniel, ready
for use.

Chant the name Haniel (HAH-KNEE-ELL) for a
minute or so. You may or may not sense the angel's
presence. If you do, continue with the next part
immediately. If you sense no presence, keep going for
a minute and *know* that Haniel can hear you.

Then say:

By the power of Raziel (RAH-ZEE-ELL),
I call on Haniel (HAH-KNEE-ELL)
to warm the heart of N.,
so that s/he feels my love
and returns it a thousandfold.
I seal this command with the word of power,
AH-RAH-REE-TAH.
It is done.

Feel a brief *Thank You*, directed toward the angel Haniel, to the spirits Jazar and Sisera, and to Raziel who has overseen the operation. You do not need to plead and beg or act as though you are inferior. These spirits are powerful, but they came because you called, and because it is their duty to serve those who call them. So, thank them politely for the results that you know you will enjoy, and know that they are dismissed and leaving you now to do their work.

The ritual is done. You can put the sigil of Haniel away and forget about the results you seek by keeping yourself busy with something else. Note that the one you love may declare passion and love within minutes, or may keep their feelings secret. Perform this ritual every day for eleven days.

Ritual 3: Creating an Aura of Attraction

This ritual will make you attractive, so much so that people will be willing to offer themselves to you. This does not mean you should sit back and wait for results, but get out there and let your attraction shine.

This is a repetition of Ritual 1, but instead of directing it to a target, you imagine yourself with hosts of beautiful people. These can be people you know, or people you simply invent for the occasion. The result is that many people will find you attractive.

In this chapter, the ritual is largely summarized. Please read the earlier ritual to understand the exact workings, feelings and methods outlined, otherwise this chapter may be ineffective.

Perform this at any time, but preferably at least three days before you want to see results.

Prepare a magickal ring as shown earlier.

Bathe or shower, as though preparing to have sex with people you desire.

Dim the lights and get naked, or dress in a way that makes you feel attractive.

Take a fresh sheet of paper and tear off a small scrap. In a circle, write the words:

Nades, Suradis, Maniner

On the other side of the scrap write these words in a circle:

Sader, Prostas, Solaster

Place this scrap of paper in the magickal ring, so that you can see the words Sader, Prostas, Solaster, and then cover them with your pyrite or other object.

Ensure that three red candles are placed nearby, but do not light them yet.

Say the following words out loud:

I am grateful for all that I have.
I am humble when I revel
in the wonders of power.

Light your three red candles. Say the following words out loud, vibrating them through your throat.

DESK-END-EE-MOOSE AB EYE-RAY

OOT ASK-END-AT ET DESK-END-AT

MOW-TOOS INT-AIR DO-OSS

NO-AH IN-WENT-AH IN LOO-KEM

IN-SEEG-NEH CORP-US
EX ELL-EM-ENT-EES

NONE EST ACK-EE-DENSE

MOON-DUSS IN MEN-SAH
MAY-AH AIR-ANT

MEESK-AIR-EH CUM

LAP-EE-DEE-BOOSE FAIR-UM

ADD KEYE-RULE-UM
WEE-REED-ESS GEM-ASS

ET WHEN-IT ET POST-HACK FOO-TOORA

NONE SUNT OWE-SA MAYA

SPECK-TOE, LOW-KUSS EST MED-EE-UM

OOT AMB-OOLS IN WEE-AH IG-NISS

TEMP-OAR-RAY MOW-EH-TOUR

Imagine the sun as a vast ball of heat and flame, shrinking to a star that moves inside your heart and resides there.

Picture yourself with many beautiful people. Masturbation can add great energy to this working. Imagine all the different kinds of people that you desire, and imagine everything from holding hands, to the most passionate sex acts. Do not hold back.

Once you feel that your passion is rising, say these spirit names:

NAH-DESS
SUE-RAH-DISS
MAH-KNEE-NAIR

Know that you are summoning spirits of lust. Repeat the names two more times, and you should feel a change in the atmosphere. If not, know that the spirits have been called and are working for you.

Visualize an orange-rosy light before you. By calling the spirits, you have summoned them to bring this light. Continue to picture glorious sex acts taking place in the rosy light, and picture yourself partaking of these sex acts. Chant the following spirit names:

SAH-DARE
PRO-STASS
SOL-AST-AIR

Speak directly to these spirits of lust, with authority, while picturing lustful situations that go exactly the way you want them to go. Picture yourself doing exactly what you desire. Continue chanting the words and continue picturing these scenes until you reach orgasm.

Wipe a small amount of your sexual fluids on the scrap of paper in the center of the ring.

To close the ritual, say the following words, vibrating each word through your throat.

WHEN-AIR-AND-UM IG-NISS
NONE TEAM-AY-OH

ET IG-NISS NONE TOH-LIT

IG-NISS CON-CORD-EE-AM FACK-EAT

Blow out the candles. The ritual is over. Repeat the ritual for five nights. At the end of the final night, dispose of the paper as described earlier. The ritual can be repeated as needed, but do not assume that frequent repetition will improve results. The initial result often lasts for some weeks, and frequent repetition is not required.

Increasing the Power

Sometimes, things don't go according to plan. If you need to ramp up the power of your magick, you can try to obtain a small personal item from the person you hope to seduce.

Ideally, this would be a hair or fingernail. If not, a thread from clothes works well. If you have to take a paperclip from the person's desk, that will work too, but the more personal the item is, the better. Be careful not to break laws or get caught.

For Ritual 1, you would place this personal item under the scrap of paper. For Ritual 2, you would simply hold onto this item during the ritual. When the rituals are complete, you dispose of this item by casting it away at a crossroads.

Some people also like to use a photograph with Ritual 1. I have not included these details in the main text, because I prefer to work with imagination, but if you find it helps, place a photograph of your target, face down underneath the scrap of paper. For some, this makes the ritual more powerful.

Seduction Magick Works

This magick works well, most of the time. If it doesn't - and on occasion, it doesn't - then be assured that you could never have gained much pleasure from the result you were seeking. Mostly, though, it works astonishingly well, and you have to live with the consequences.

Love and sex generate powerful emotions. Be aware that every time you seduce, you are connecting with another soul, and your own emotions may be dragged into the magick.

These are mild warnings, though. So long as you are kind, this is just about the most fun you can have. Seduction magick is a joy for you and for those you seduce.

If you have questions, our website is an excellent source of background material and practical posts that help you to get magick working.

We could have published two or three books on magickal practice, but instead, it's all there for free. You can also find extensive FAQs for every book. I urge you to make good use of the site when you encounter problems, and also when you wish to expand your understanding of magick.

There are new posts every few weeks, and they can help keep your magick vital and hone your understanding.

The Gallery of Magick Facebook page will also keep you up to date. Please note that we only have one official Facebook page, and information in various fan groups is not always accurate.

If you have an interest in developing your magick further, there are many texts that can assist you, covering everything from money magic to archangels and demons. Please visit our website to find out more.

Damon Brand

www.galleryofmagick.com

Printed in Great Britain
by Amazon

76184652R00031